T0143699

Printed in the USA
CPSIA information can be obtained
at www.ICGtesting.com
JSHW060947120824
67981JS00005B/60

9 780867 050554

שַׁ בָּת

Shin שׁ

Complete the Shin.

Practice writing the Shin.

Put an X on each picture that does **not** belong to Shabbat.

Lesson
1
Shin

Color in the picture
that starts with
the sound of ש.

Circle each Shin.

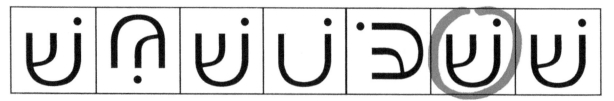

Lesson **1** **Sh**in

Color in each space that has a picture beginning with the שׁ sound.

What is the sound of the letter you now see? _____

Who is saying the שׁ sound?
Write the Hebrew letter in the correct box.

Lesson **2** **B**et

ב ית

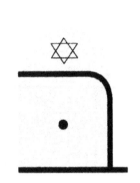

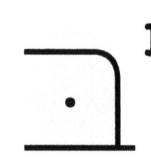

Bet ב

Complete the Bet.

Practice writing the Bet.

ב

Color the fruit that begins with the new sound.

BEST BUYS ON FRUIT FOR SHABBAT

25¢   60¢   59¢

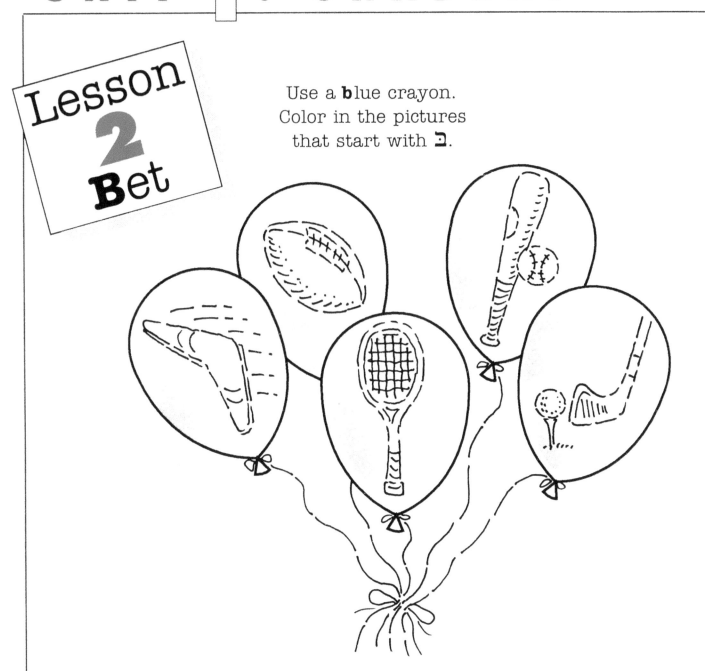

Lesson 2 Bet

Use a **b**lue crayon.
Color in the pictures
that start with בּ.

Circle the letters that match each picture.

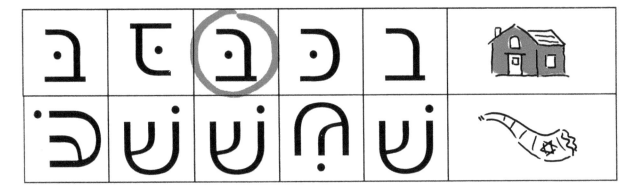

Lesson 2 Bet

Help each Hebrew letter
find its English friend.

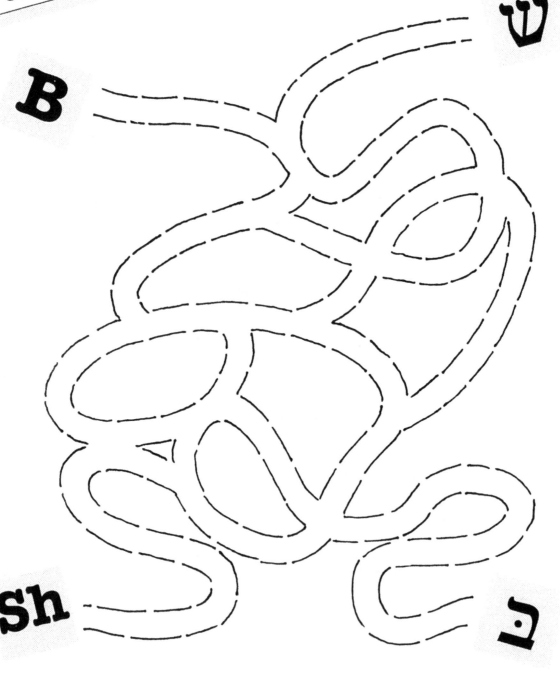

ת ורה

Tav ת or ת

Complete the Tav.

Practice writing the Tav.

Lesson 3 Tav

Find another picture that starts with ת.
Draw a line from the letter to that picture.

On each line circle the Hebrew letters that match the English sound.

SH	ת	ת	שׁ	כ	שׁ	כ	(שׁ)
B	ת	כ	שׁ	ת	שׁ	ת	כ
T	ת	כ	ת	כ	שׁ	ת	שׁ

Lesson 3 Tav

Color the sound of

Sh in brown
B in blue
T in yellow

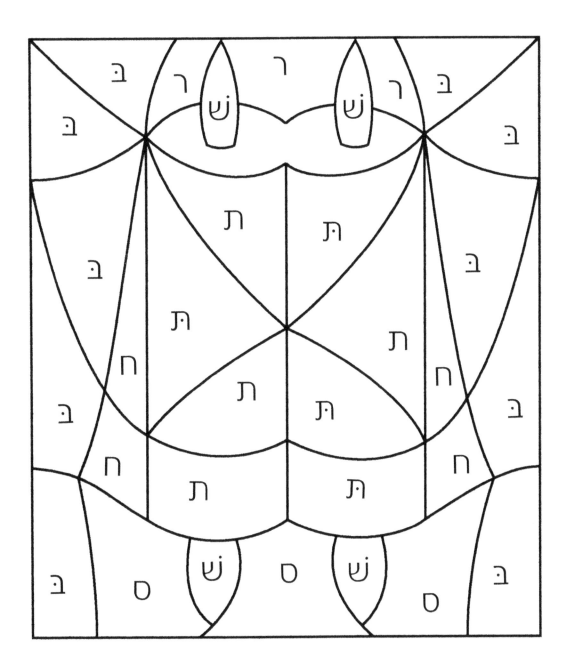

Lesson 3 Tav

What Hebrew letter does each picture start with? Write the Hebrew letter below each picture.

On the challah cover below, write the Hebrew word Shabbat.

Lesson
4
Nun

נ רות

Nun   נ

Complete the Nun.

1 ↓

ג ג ג ג ג ג ג ג ג ג

Practice the Nun.

ג

Find the new sound. Color in the picture.

שבת

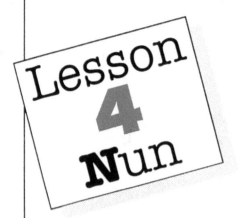

Lesson 4 Nun

Connect the matching letters.

ת   שׁ
תשׁ............... בּ
ת   ת
נ   נ
בּ

Circle the letter that matches each picture.

ת   בּ

בּ   שׁ

נ   שׁ

ת   נ

Lesson 4 Nun

Make the Shabbat flowers beautiful. Color in each petal that has a letter to match the picture.

Your teacher will tell you how to do this page.

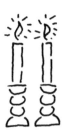

Lesson **5** **L**amed

ל וח

Lamed ל

Complete the Lamed.

Practice the Lamed.

Find which objects start with the new sound. Color them in.

Lesson
5
Lamed

Color in each
Lamed. How
many did you
find? _____

Write the first letter of each child's name
in Hebrew on the notebooks.

Nathan
_____

Sharon
שׁ
_____

Tammy
_____

Leah
_____

Ben
_____

16

Lesson 5 Lamed

Circle the Hebrew letter that begins each picture.

בּ	ת	נ	בּ	(תּ)	שׁ		
נ	ל	שׁ	נ	תּ	ל		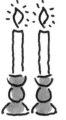
בּ	שׁ	ל	תּ	שׁ	תּ		
תּ	בּ	נ	תּ	ל	בּ		
ל	תּ	תּ	ל	שׁ	נ		

ג יר

Gimel

ג

Complete the Gimel.

Practice the Gimel.

ג

Color the animal **green** that starts with the sound of ג.

Lesson 6 Gimel

On each camel color in the packages with the Hebrew letters that match the English letters.

Lesson **6** **G**imel

What Hebrew letter
does it start with?

ש‍ַ

Lesson 7 Samech

S ס פ ר

Samech ס

Complete the Samech.

Practice the Samech.

ס

Find the new sound.

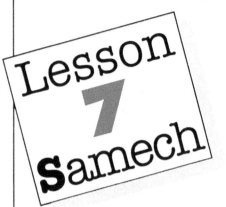

Lesson 7 Samech

Connect the matching letters within each box.

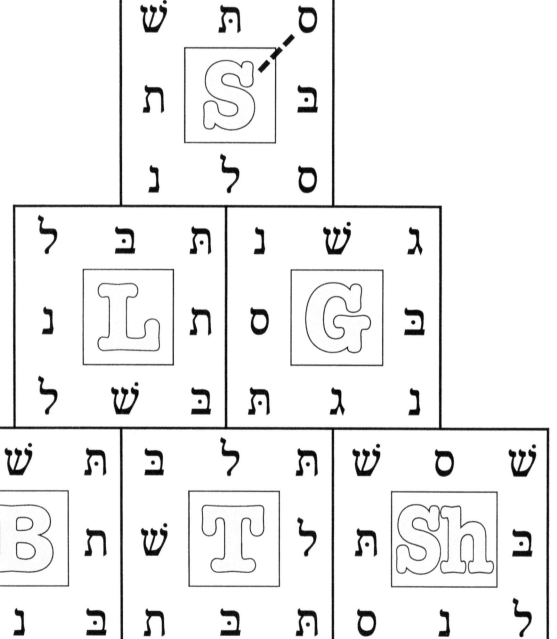

Lesson 7 Samech

Fill in the pages in each book. Write the Hebrew letter and draw a picture for each letter.

Sh

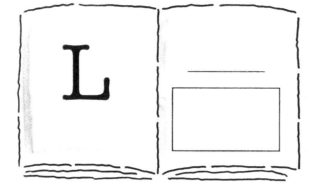

L

T

N

B

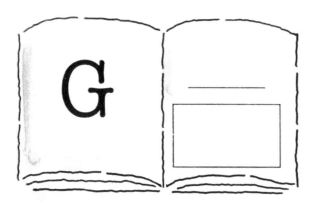

G

S

Lesson 7 Samech

Help the children find their backpacks.

Circle the child with the lost bag.

Guess the child's name: _____

Lesson **8** **V**av

ו ו

Vav ו

Complete the Vav.

1

Practice the Vav.

ו

Find the picture that begins with the new sound.
Color it in.

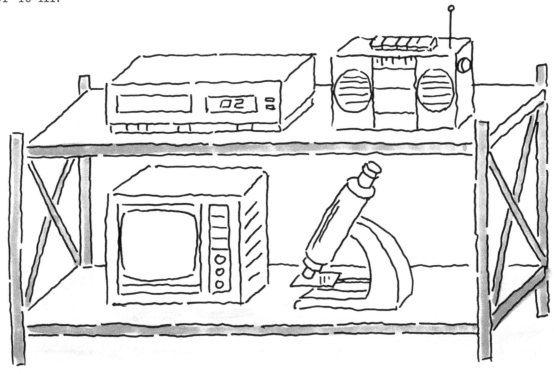

Lesson
8
Vav

Draw a line from each picture
to the letter it begins with.

ל ג ו

שׁ ס ל

נ ס ג

נ ו ג

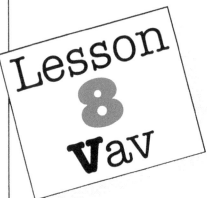

Lesson **8** Vav

Find the "twins" in each row.
Then draw a picture of something
that starts with that letter.

ו ג ל (שׁ) ס (שׁ)	〜
ו ת נ ו ב ג	
נ ת ב שׁ ת ג	
ל ג נ ס נ ו	
נ ת ב ג ו ג	

Help the kids find their caps.

Your teacher will tell you how to do this page.

Lesson 9 Chet

ח תול
Chet ח

Complete the Chet.

Practice the Chet.

ח

Which path will take the cat to a food that starts with the new Hebrew sound?

Lesson
9
Chet

Color in anything that starts with ח.

Circle the letters that match.

						ח
ת	ח	ת	ת	ח	נ	
נ	ו	ג	נ	ו	ג	נ
ג	נ	ו	ג	נ	ו	ו
ו	ג	נ	ו	ג	נ	ג
ת	ח	ו	ת	ח	ו	ת

Lesson 9 Chet

Connect each cat with its mouse.

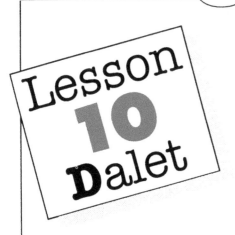

ד ג

Dalet ד

Complete the Dalet.

Practice writing the Dalet.

Color:

D in yellow
B in blue
V in pink
G in green

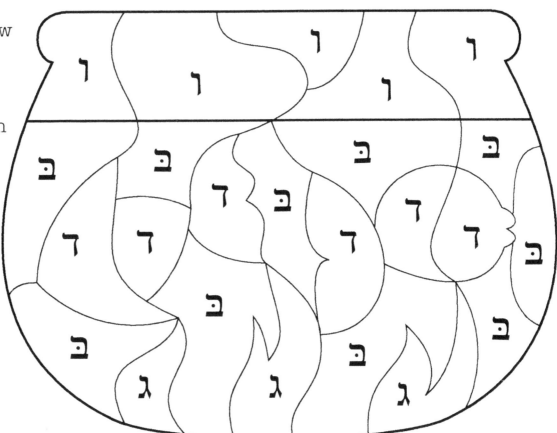

Lesson 10 Dalet

Guy	
Dina	
Sam	
Leah	
Velvel	

Which fish won the race? _____

Who came in second? _____

Who came in third? _____

Write the first Hebrew letter of the winners' names in the boxes.

The losers just get ribbons. Sorry! Write the first Hebrew letter of their names.

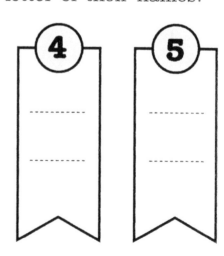

Lesson
10
Dalet

Connect the pictures that start with
the same sound. Write the letter
they start with in the box.

Lesson 11 Koph

ק נגרו

Koph ק

Complete the Koph.

Practice writing the Koph.

Color in anything that starts with ק.

Hebrew Tic-Tac-Toe

Play these Tic-Tac-Toe games with a friend. Draw an X or an O on a letter you know. Say a Hebrew word that starts with that letter.

SQUARE 1

שׁ	גּ	ל
ס	ח	דּ
ק	בּ	תּ

SQUARE 2

נ	ס	ק
תּ	ו	ח
ל	ד	גּ

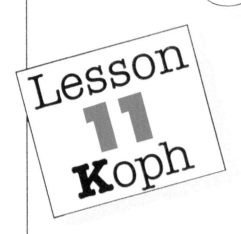

Lesson 11 Koph

Circle two pictures that start with the same sound. Write the Hebrew letter on the line.

Lesson 12 Zayin

ז ברה

Zayin ז

Complete the Zayin.

Practice writing the Zayin.

Use a black crayon. Color in the stripes with
the letter that makes the sound of **Z**.

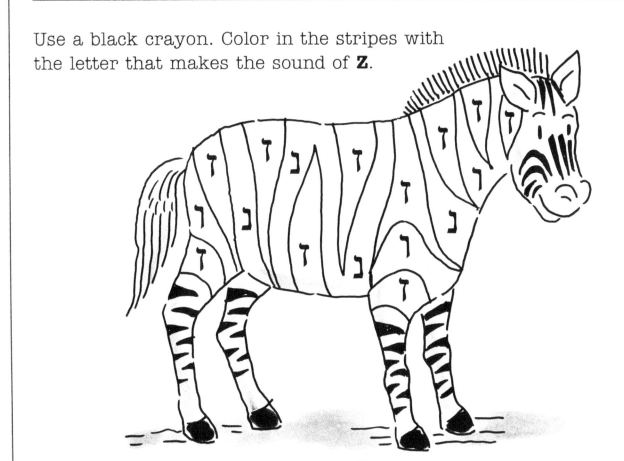

Lesson 12 Zayin

Draw a path from each cat to its bowl.

Sammy

Karen

Dumpy

Zebra

Lesson 12 Zayin

Find the odd one out and write the Hebrew letter it starts with in the box.

Lesson 12 Zayin

Find the twins in each row.
Then draw a picture of something
that starts with that letter.

נ	ו	ג	ז	ד	ו	
ח	נ	ב	ח	ג	ת	
נ	ד	ג	ו	ג	ז	
ז	ד	נ	ג	ו	ד	
ס	ש	ו	ס	נ	ג	
ל	ת	ק	ח	ק	ב	
ז	ס	נ	ג	ו	ז	
ח	ל	ק	ס	ל	ש	

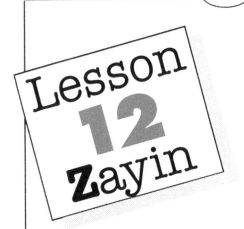

Lesson 12 Zayin

You be the teacher! If the Hebrew letter in a square below is correct, put a check next to it. If the Hebrew letter is not correct, write the correct letter.

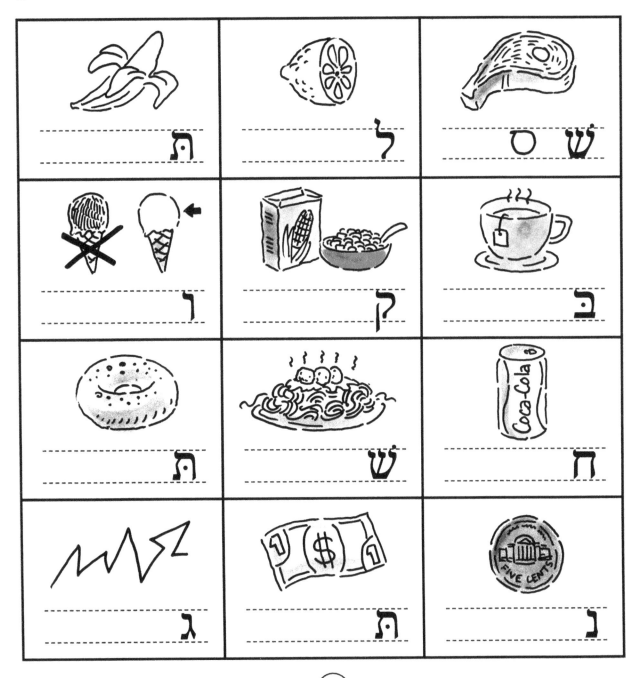

Your teacher will tell you how to do this page.

Lesson 13 Pey

פ סח

Pey פ

Complete the Pey.

Practice writing the Pey.

פ

Cross out the things that **don't** belong on the Pesach table.
Color in the rest.

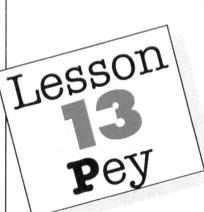

Lesson
13
Pey

Color:

P   in brown

D   in red

K   in green

Z   in yellow

B   in blue

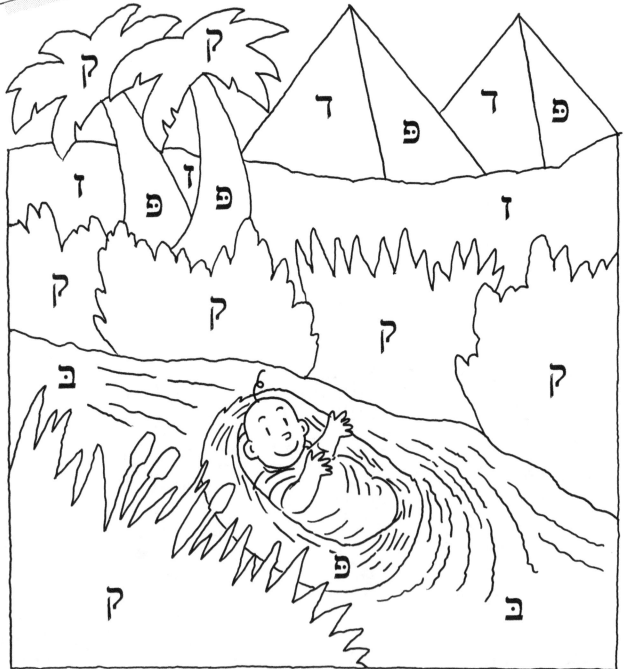

Lesson 13 Pey

Circle the picture that starts with a **different** sound. Write the letter it starts with in the center.

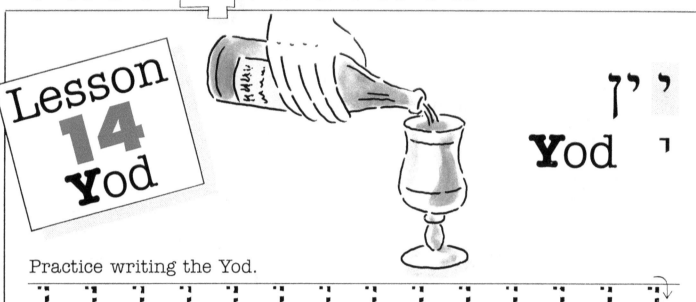

Lesson **14** **Y**od

ייַן

Yod י

Practice writing the Yod.

יֽ   יֽ   יֽ   יֽ   יֽ   יֽ   יֽ   יֽ   יֽ   יֽ   יֽ   יֽ ↓

Color in the object that starts with the new sound.

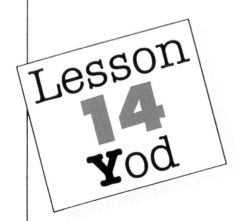

Lesson 14 Yod

Help Levi, David, Shelley, and Benny find their glasses. Write each name in English under the correct wine glass.

Now fill up the glasses with wine:
Levi likes a full glass.
David wants just a little bit.
Benny wants a half glass.
Shelley wants orange juice instead of wine.

49

Lesson
14
Yod

Connect the letters to the pictures that match.

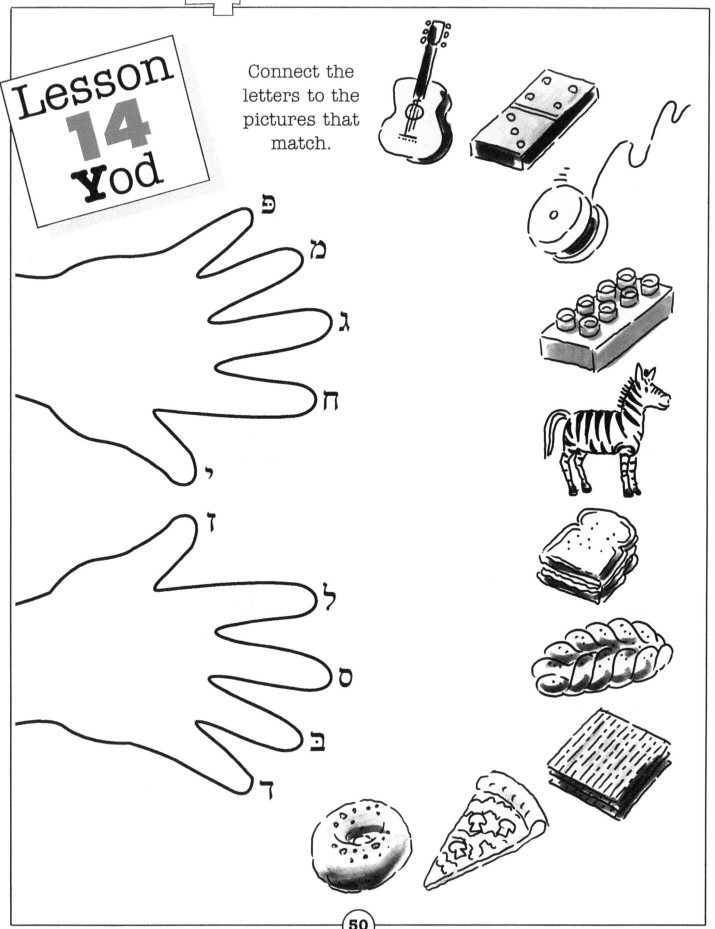

פ
מ
ג
ח
י
ז
ל
ס
ב
ד

Lesson 15 Mem

מ צה

Mem מ

מם!

Complete the Mem.

Practice writing the Mem.

מ

Whose name starts with the new sound? Color that picture.

Lesson 15 Mem

Little Red Riding Hood is packing a basket for Savta (Grandma) for Pesach. She used a Hebrew code for her shopping list:

SHOPPING LIST מ י ר פ ס

Color in the items you think are on the list. Cross out the other ones. (Hint: Banana = בּ)

Lesson
15
Mem

Connect the letter to the matching pictures. Cross out the odd ones.

Lesson 16 Hey

ה גדה

Hey   ה

Complete the Hey.

הּ ה ה ה ה ה ה ה ה ה

Practice writing the Hey.

ה

How many hidden Heys can you find? _____
Color them in with different colors.

Connect the nameplates and the Haggadot, and decorate each הגדה.

Peggy Z.

Yossi L.

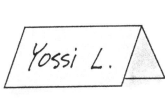

Michael P.

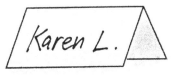

Karen L.

Helen Y.

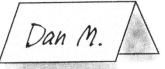

Dan M.

Lesson 16 Hey

Mah Nishtanah?

At the seder the youngest child asks 4 questions.
Circle the 2 matching Hebrew letters in each shape.
Write the English sound on the line below.

UNIT : PESACH

Lesson 16 Hey

Circle the two pictures on each line that start with the same sound. Write the Hebrew letter they start with.

Your teacher will tell you how to do this page.

Lesson 17 Resh

ר בְּי

Resh ר

Complete the Resh.

Practice writing the Resh.

What is the רַבִּי doing in these pictures?

Lesson
17
Resh

Mom used her secret Hebrew code to choose gifts for a wedding and a Bar Mitzvah. What do you think she chose for each?
ד ו ס מ פ י ג ת ר ב Fill in the chart:

Wedding		Bar Mitzvah	
1. Dollars	ת	1.	
2.		2.	
3.		3.	
4.		4.	
5.		5.	

Lesson 17 Resh

In each row 2 pictures end with the same letter. Write that end letter in the box on the right. Cross out the picture that doesn't match.

Lesson 18 Kaph

כ פה

Kaph כ

Complete the Kaph.

Practice the Kaph.

כ

Who needs a כפה? Draw one where needed.

Lesson 18 Kaph

Color the sound of

R in red
M in brown
K in tan
H in blue
P in yellow
G in green

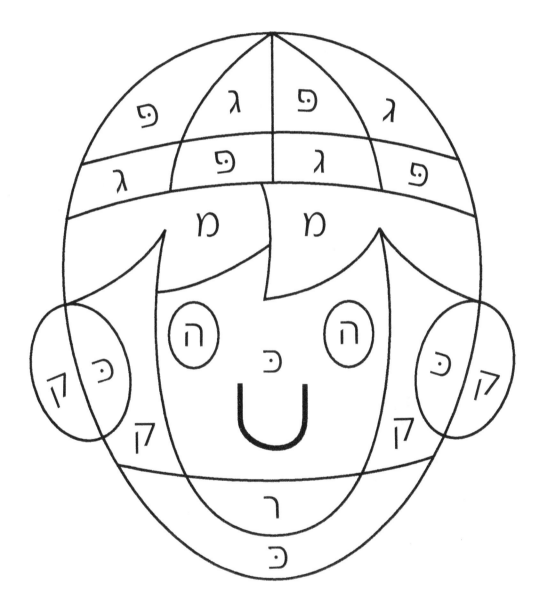

What is this boy wearing on his head? _____

Lesson 18 Kaph

Kaph means

Help the babies find their spoons.

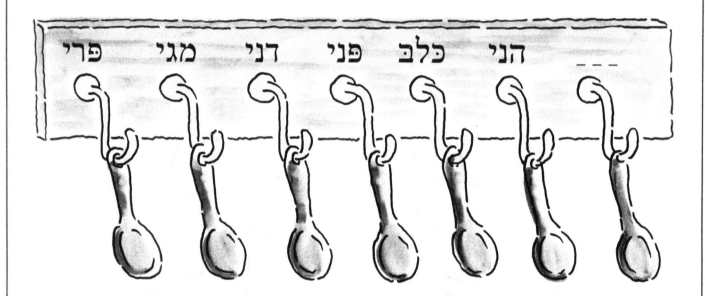

פרי מגי דני פני כלב הני ___

Maggy Danny Molly Perry Henny Penny Caleb

Whose spoon is missing a name? Write it in.

Lesson 18 Kaph

Get me to the synagogue on time!
Race a friend and see who gets there first.
Your teacher will tell you how to play.

Lesson 19 Tet

ט לית

Tet ט

Complete the Tet.

ט ט ט ט ט ט ט ט ט ט ט ט ט ט ט

Practice the Tet.

ט

Color in the sections with the sound of **T**.

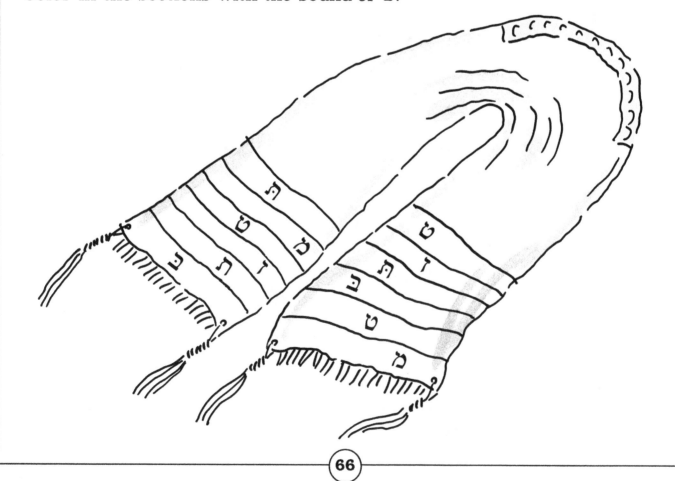

Lesson
19
Tet

Connect the picture to a letter.

Circle the letters that make the sound of the English letter in each row.

B	כ	מ	⬤ב	כ	⬤ב
S	שׁ	ס	שׁ	ס	ז
D	ד	ר	ד	ת	ר
H	ה	ח	ה	ח	ק
T	ד	ט	ב	ט	ת
P	ב	כ	פ	פ	ב
K	ל	ק	ב	כ	ל
R	ר	ד	ו	ד	ר
M	מ	ט	מ	ט	פ

Lesson 19 Tet

Help each Rabbi find a kipah and tallit.
Draw a line from the Rabbi to the tallit
and from the Rabbi to the kipah.

Rabbi
David
Shore

Rabbi
Moshe
Tucker

Rabbi
Tal
Davis

Rabbi
Shelly
Dubin

Rabbi
Teddy
Marx

Lesson 20 Tsadi

צ דקה

Tsadi   צ

Complete the Tsadi.

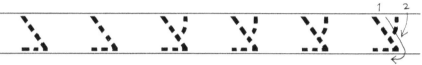

Practice the Tsadi.

צ

Where does Tsedakah money go?
Draw a circle around the correct pictures.

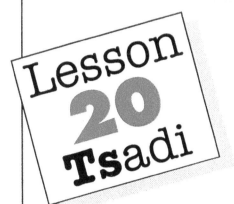

Lesson 20 Tsadi

Using a ruler, draw lines between the letters that make the same sound.

R ר   ק כ

G נ ר S ג   D ו K ד Z

פ   P

      B   ב

י N L ס Y   M V ט מ ז

ל L   ת T

Lesson
20
Tsadi

In each row 3 of the 4 objects start with the same sound. Circle the odd object in each row. What Hebrew letter does it start with? Write that letter on the right.

ח

Tic-Tac-Toe Plus

Your teacher will tell you how to play this game.

כ	ת	ה	כ	דג	צ
ר	צ	ל	ב	מ	נ
ו	ס	שבת	פ	ט	ג
ט	שׁ	ז	ס	פסח	ק
ח	רבי	כ	ת	ק	ח
נ	י	ו	ר	ד	ה

UNIT : VOCABULARY

Your teacher will tell you how to do this page and the next page.

שַׁבָּת

בַּכִּתָּה

בַּבַּיִת

פסח

בית כנסת

Lesson 21
Aleph/Ayin

Aleph אַ א
Ayin עַ ע

Complete the Aleph.

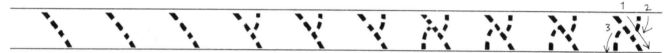

Complete the Ayin.

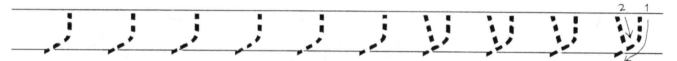

The silent letters are hiding. Color in the ones you can find.

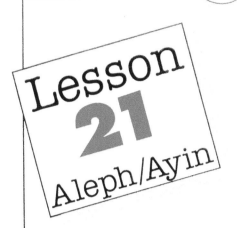

Lesson
21
Aleph/Ayin

Color in the spaces with the silent pictures.

What two letters do you see? _____

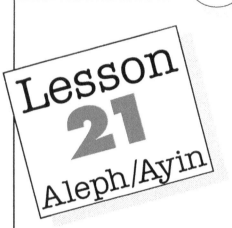

Lesson
21
Aleph/Ayin

Circle the pictures that start with a vowel sound.

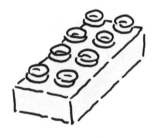

The first letter in all these words is the letter Aleph.
Write that letter. _____

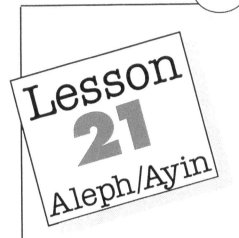

Lesson 21
Aleph/Ayin

Help the detective!
Listen to the words and
connect the pictures
that start with the
same sound.

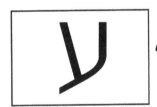

All the words on the right start with an Aleph. Write it here. ____
All the words on the left start with an Ayin. Write it here. ____

PRESENTED TO

_____

who has completed the program

קָדִימָה!

GET READY FOR
HEBREW!

School_____

Teacher_____

Date_____